DINOSAURS OF EDEN

A BIBLICAL JOURNEY THROUGH TIME

Ken Ham

Illustrated By
Earl & Bonita Snellenberger

OLD TESTAMENT

Master Books

First printing, March 2001
Fifth printing, January 2006

For more information write: Master Books, Inc.
P. O. Box 726, Green Forest, AR 72638

Please visit our web site for other great titles:
www.masterbooks.net

ISBN 13: 978-0-89051-340-8
ISBN 10: 0-89051-340-6

Library of Congress: 00-110205

Printed in the United States of America

PURPOSES OF THE BOOK

This book has been written to instruct readers about dinosaurs and to teach them to think with a Christian world view that is founded in the Bible. They will learn that Christianity is based in *real* history, and that the Bible is not *just* a book about salvation, but is THE HISTORY BOOK OF THE UNIVERSE. This will also enable readers to know how to understand and defend the gospel.

DEDICATION

This book is dedicated to the precious children of the world, who all need to hear the wonderful truths from God's Holy Word.

ABOUT THE AUTHOR

A founder and current executive director of the Bible-upholding ministry of *Answers in Genesis*, Ken Ham is one of the most in-demand Christian speakers in North America. A native Australian now residing near Cincinnati, Ohio, he is the author (or co-author) of numerous books and articles on the authority of the Bible beginning with Genesis (*The Lie: Evolution*), dinosaurs (*The Great Dinosaur Mystery Solved*), and the evil fruits of evolutionary thinking (the new book on the origin of "races" and racism, *One Blood*).

Ken is also the host of a daily radio program called "Answers . . . with Ken Ham," heard on over 450 outlets worldwide, and is the head of the team that is building a large creation museum west of the Cincinnati airport. For information, go to *Answers in Genesis Ministries* web site: www.AnswersInGenesis.org, or write to *Answers in Genesis*:

P.O. Box 6330	P.O. Box 6302	5-420 Erb Street West, Suite 213	P.O. Box 5262
Florence, KY 41022	Acacia Ridge DC, Qld 4110	Waterloo, Ontario N2L 6K6	Leicester, LE2 3XU
USA	AUSTRALIA	CANADA	UNITED KINGDOM

ACKNOWLEDGMENT

I wish to thank my beloved wife, Mally, and our five dear children, who patiently and willingly allow me the time to write books such as this. I also wish to thank my assistant, David Jolly, for helping to coordinate this project with artists Earl and Bonita Snellenberger and Master Books.

Ken Ham

Have you ever imagined what it would be like if there really were such a thing as a time machine? We could go back in history and see Solomon's Temple, for example. Now that would be incredible! Or we could watch Noah build the Ark. Imagine if we could see the Garden of Eden before sin; it must have been much more beautiful than we could ever imagine.

And what about DINOSAURS? Wouldn't it be just fantastic to go back in history and see a real *T. rex* and find out when it lived, what it ate, how it behaved?

Even though we don't have a time machine, we have something that is far better. We have a written record of the history of the universe, past, present and future, from someone who sees and knows EVERYTHING!

Even if we had a time machine, however, we wouldn't understand which events of history were the most important for us to know about. You see, we might go to one place at a particular time, but not know that something was happening in another location which was vital for us to know about.

But, the infinite Creator of the universe made sure that all the most important events of history were recorded in a special series of books that together make up one book, the Bible. In a sense, reading the Bible is like traveling in a time machine.

In fact, we could call the Bible "**THE HISTORY BOOK OF THE UNIVERSE.**" It is the ONLY 100 percent accurate history book in the world! Using the Bible, we can travel into the past and also into the future.

You are going to learn how this "time machine" — The History Book of the Universe (the Bible) — enables us to understand all about dinosaurs: when they lived, what they ate, why we find their bones, what happened to them, and much more!

You are going on a journey through the BIBLE TIME-GATE!

Before you read on, look up the following verses in the Bible that will help you understand that the Bible really is very special. It IS the Word of God, who ALWAYS tells the truth, and who has always existed. Studying God's Word is the only way we will know the truth about the past concerning dinosaurs.

Bible memory verses: 1 Thessalonians 2:13; 2 Peter 1:19–21; 2 Timothy 3:14–16; Psalm 119:160; Proverbs 30:5–6; Hebrews 4:12; 2 Timothy 2:15.

What do these verses have to do with creatures like a *Dilophosaurus* or *Cryolophosaurus*?

Bible memory verse: *All scripture is given by inspiration of God, and is profitable for doctrine, for reproof, for correction, for instruction in righteousness* (2 Timothy 3:16).

You have probably heard of dinosaurs like *Triceratops*, *Styracosaurus*, or *Tyrannosaurus rex*. (By the way, we know dinosaurs once existed, because we find their bones — sometimes whole skeletons — in the earth.) And you have no doubt read or heard such things as: "dinosaurs lived millions of years ago"; "the disappearance of the dinosaurs is a big mystery"; "dinosaurs aren't mentioned in the Bible"; "dinosaurs were not created, they evolved"; and so on.

Cryolophosaurus
(cry-o-LOF-o-SAWR-us)
meaning "frozen crested reptile."

Dilophosaurus
(die-LOF-o-SAWR-us),
meaning "two-crested reptile."

Styracosaurus
(sty-RAK-o-SAWR-us),
meaning "spiked reptile."

Tyrannosaurus rex
(ti-RAN-oh-SAWR-us rex),
meaning "tyrant reptile king."

First of all, put out of your mind all these ideas you have heard about dinosaurs. Instead, let us get into our "time machine" (the Bible) and travel back to the beginning of history, and even to the beginning of time itself.

The first verse in the first book (Genesis) of the Bible states: ***In the beginning God created the heaven and the earth.*** God, who has always existed (no one made God, for He made EVERYTHING), tells us in this first verse that He made time (beginning), space (heaven), and matter (earth). This was the beginning of our universe, all part of the first day in time.

Triceratops
(trie-SER-a-tops),
meaning "three-horned face."

As you read the first chapter of Genesis, you discover that God gives us a summary of what happened on each of the six days of Creation. Day 1: time, space, Earth, light; Day 2: atmosphere; Day 3: the dry land appeared and God made the plants; Day 4: God created the sun, moon, and stars; Day 5: God created the sea creatures and the flying creatures; Day 6: God created the land animals and the first two people — Adam and Eve.

By the way, some people think that the six days of Creation were not ordinary days as we know them, but were long periods of time. This is wrong. The Hebrew word for "day" (*yom*) always means an ordinary day when it is used with the words "evening" or "morning," or used with a number. When you read Genesis chapter 1, you will see that the word "day" is used with "evening," "morning," *and* number for each of the six days. This means they must have been ORDINARY days as we know them. They were not long periods or millions of years.

Let's read Exodus 20:11:

For in six days the LORD made heaven and earth, the sea, and all that in them is, and rested the seventh day: wherefore the LORD blessed the sabbath day, and hallowed it.

This is part of the Ten Commandments that God himself wrote on stone (Exodus 31:18). This verse tells us why we have a seven-day week: God worked for six days (when He created everything) and rested for one. This is where our seven-day week comes from! If God created everything in six long periods (or millions of years), our week would be millions of years long! That wouldn't make any sense whatsoever.

Now you might be saying, "What has all this got to do with dinosaurs?"

Bible memory verse: *And he gave unto Moses, when he had made an end of communing with him upon mount Sinai, two tables of testimony, tables of stone, written with the finger of God* (Exodus 31:18).

In the Bible, in the Book of Colossians, we read that God (through His Son, Jesus Christ) created EVERYTHING:

For by him were all things created, that are in heaven, and that are in earth (Colossians 1:16).

We know that dinosaurs once existed on Earth (we find their bones, which we will discuss later), so God **must have** created dinosaurs. An Englishman, Sir Richard Owen, invented the word "dinosaur" in 1841. He had the bones of two creatures called *Iguanodon* and *Megalosaurus*, and he realized these were from a group of animals different from any other group he had studied. Owen recognized that they needed a special name. As these bones came from very large types of reptiles that lived on the land, he made up the word "dinosaur," which means "terrible lizard."

So the word "dinosaurs" refers to a special group of reptiles that lived on the land. Now, on what day did God make the land animals? Day 6 of the Creation week. Since God created everything, and since He created land animals on Day 6 (an ordinary day) — and dinosaurs were land animals — then dinosaurs were made on the sixth day of Creation!

And God said, Let the earth bring forth the living creature after their kind, cattle, and creeping thing, and beast of the earth after his kind: and it was so (Genesis 1:24).

But that's not all God did on Day 6. Genesis 1:27 states:

So God created man in his own image, in the image of God created he him; male and female created he them.

Sir Richard Owen, famed anatomist and founder of the British Museum of Natural History, originated the name Dinosauria.

Based upon the few fossil remains of Iguanodon *found at first, Sir Richard Owen mistakenly placed a thumb spike on its snout in this early reconstruction.*

The first two people, Adam and Eve, were ALSO made on the sixth day of Creation. Do you know what this means? We can say, 100 percent, absolutely for sure, that people lived with dinosaurs! The reason we can be so sure is that God, who doesn't tell a lie, told us in His Word that land animals and Adam and Eve were made on the sixth day of Creation!

Bible memory verse: *God is not a man, that he should lie* (Numbers 23:19).

And now we need to answer another very important question: How long ago was it that God created the land animals and Adam and Eve In Genesis 5:3–11, we read the following:

And Adam lived an hundred and thirty years, and begat a son in his own likeness, after his image; and called his name Seth: And the days of Adam after he had begotten Seth were eight hundred years: and he begat sons and daughters: And all the days that Adam lived were nine hundred and thirty years: and he died. And Seth lived an hundred and five years, and begat Enos: And Seth lived after he begat Enos eight hundred and seven years, and begat sons and daughters: And all the days of Seth were nine hundred and twelve years and he died. And Enos lived ninety years, and begat Cainan: And Enos lived after he begat Cainan eight hundred and fifteen years, and begat sons and daughters: And all the days of Enos were nine hundred and five years: and he died.

Have you ever wondered why lists like this that tell us about when people had children, and when they died, are all through the Bible? Well, God did this so we could trace the history of the world back to the beginning! When we add up all these dates, and the dates of other events given in the Bible, we find that God created the universe around 6,000 years ago.

This means that Adam and Eve, and the dinosaurs, were also created about 6,000 years ago!

Heterodontosaurus
(HET-er-o-DONT-o-SAWR-us), *meaning "reptile with different teeth."*

Megalosaurus
(MEG-a-lo-SAWR-us),
*meaning "big reptile,"
was the first dinosaur
to be named scientifically.*

Iguanodon
(i-GWAHN-o-don),
*meaning "iguana tooth,"
was the second dinosaur
to be named scientifically.*

Scutellosaurus
(skoo-TEL-o-SAWR-us),
meaning "small scaled reptile."

This is a totally different view of history from the one we usually see on television, read in newspapers, or hear in almost all schools. Most of us are constantly bombarded with the idea that dinosaurs lived millions of years before people. Later, we will see why this evolutionary view of history is **not correct** at all. When we believe God, who was there, then the truth is that dinosaurs and people first came into existence only *thousands* of years ago.

Why then do we not find the word "dinosaur" in the Bible?

Bible memory verse: *Where wast thou when I laid the foundations of the earth? declare, if thou hast understanding* (Job 38:4).

The Bible verses in this book are all from the King James Version, which was translated from Greek and Hebrew into English in 1611. The word "dinosaur" was not coined until 1841. That's why you won't find the word "dinosaur" in this translation. You might be wondering: What were dinosaurs called before the word was invented?

Read the following passages from the Bible and see if you can guess:

*. . . and it shall be an habitation of **dragons*** (Isaiah 34:13)

*. . . the **dragons** of the wilderness* (Malachi 1:3)

*. . . they snuffed up the wind like **dragons*** (Jeremiah 14:6)

It is interesting to note that the word "dragon" occurs a number of times in the Old Testament, and when you replace it with the word "dinosaur," in most instances it seems to fit very nicely.

We have all heard of the word "dragon," and we are familiar with dragon legends from around the world. For instance, some legends tell us the Chinese bred dragons. Many of the descriptions of these "dragons" really do fit the descriptions of some of the dinosaurs we all know about.

In a glass case in the British Museum in London, there is a very old history book, the *Anglo-Saxon Chronicles*, that records events that occurred nearly 1,000 years ago. In this book there are accounts of dragons that lived beside people. The fascinating thing is that the descriptions of these dragons fit the dinosaurs.

Kentrosaurus
(KEN-tro-SAWR-us),
meaning "prickly reptile."

The flag of the country of Wales

The country of Wales has the picture of a dragon on its flag. Maybe the story about St. George fighting a dragon is really an account of a fight with a dinosaur!

So dragons were most likely what we call dinosaurs today!

Did dragons only live on the land?

Bible memory verse: *It is better to trust in the Lord than to put confidence in man* (Psalm 118:8).

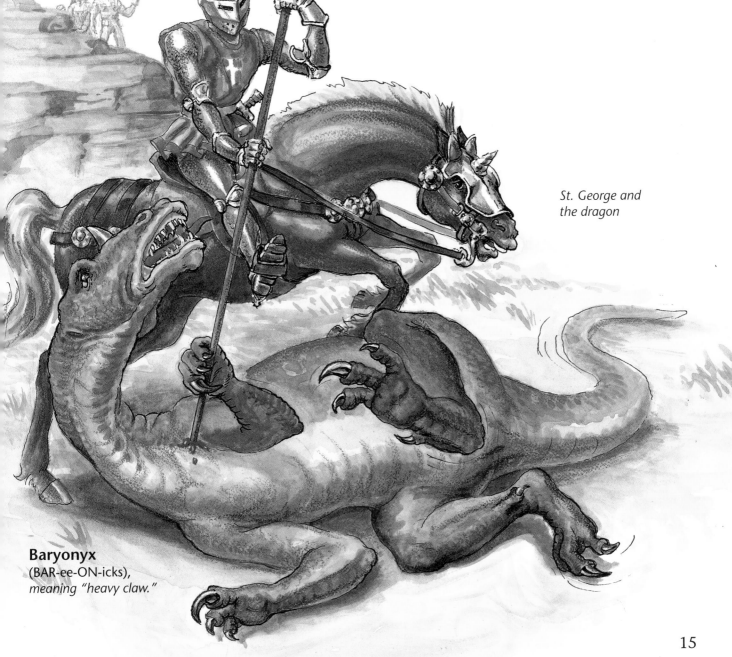

St. George and the dragon

Baryonyx
(BAR-ee-ON-icks),
meaning "heavy claw."

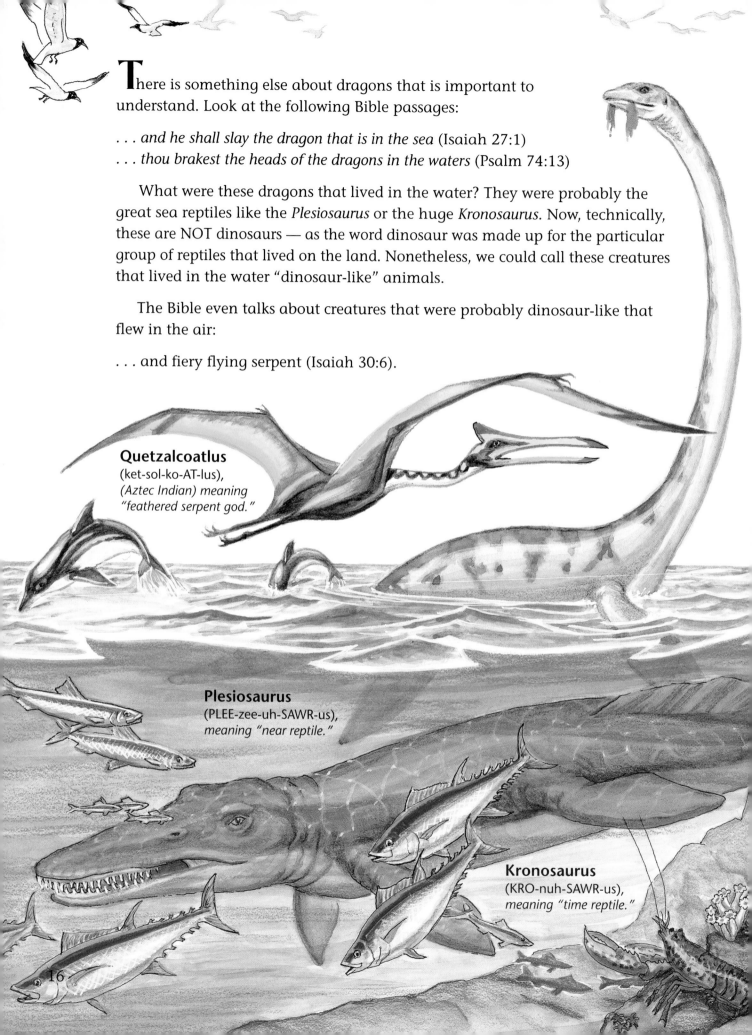

There is something else about dragons that is important to understand. Look at the following Bible passages:

. . . and he shall slay the dragon that is in the sea (Isaiah 27:1)
. . . thou brakest the heads of the dragons in the waters (Psalm 74:13)

What were these dragons that lived in the water? They were probably the great sea reptiles like the *Plesiosaurus* or the huge *Kronosaurus*. Now, technically, these are NOT dinosaurs — as the word dinosaur was made up for the particular group of reptiles that lived on the land. Nonetheless, we could call these creatures that lived in the water "dinosaur-like" animals.

The Bible even talks about creatures that were probably dinosaur-like that flew in the air:

. . . and fiery flying serpent (Isaiah 30:6).

Quetzalcoatlus
(ket-sol-ko-AT-lus),
(Aztec Indian) meaning
"feathered serpent god."

Plesiosaurus
(PLEE-zee-uh-SAWR-us),
meaning "near reptile."

Kronosaurus
(KRO-nuh-SAWR-us),
meaning "time reptile."

Pteranodon
(tair-AN-o-don),
meaning "winged and toothless."

Rhamphorhynchus
(ram-fo-RINK-us),
meaning "narrow beak."

This may be a reference to the flying reptiles such as *Pteranodon* or *Rhamphorhynchus*.

These sea dwelling and flying reptiles were made on the fifth day of Creation, as we read about in Genesis 1:20–21:

And God said, Let the waters bring forth abundantly the moving creature that hath life, and fowl that may fly above the earth in the open firmament of heaven. And God created great whales, and every living creature that moveth, which the waters brought forth abundantly, after their kind, and every winged fowl after his kind: and God saw that it was good.

It's important for you to understand that from the original written Hebrew language of Genesis, the word translated into English as "whales" actually is the word "dragons," the sea reptiles. Also, the word translated "fowl" doesn't just mean birds; in the Hebrew language, this word means any flying creature and would include the flying reptiles as well as birds.

When we study the Bible very carefully, isn't it fascinating what we find? God's Word is full of all sorts of information many people don't know about, but all need to hear!

Did you know the Bible even tells us what dinosaurs originally ate?

Bible memory verse: *Every word of God is pure* (Proverbs 30:5).

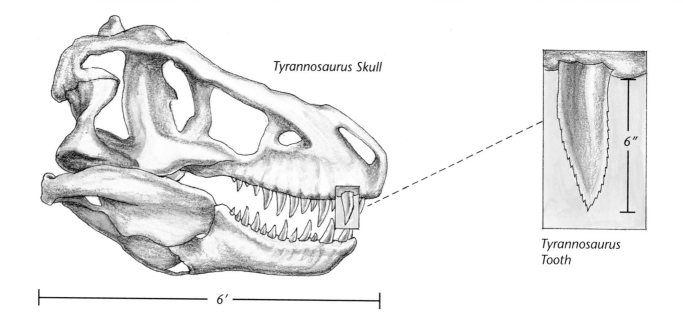

Tyrannosaurus Skull

Tyrannosaurus Tooth

6"

6'

Have you ever been to a museum and seen the skull, jaw, and teeth of a large *Tyrannosaurus rex*? What a jaw! Six feet long, filled with teeth up to six inches long! This certainly makes you wonder what *T. rex* ate: other animals, people, anything he wanted to?

Now this may come as a surprise, but we do know what *T. rex* ate originally — and it wasn't animals or people. It was plants. Let's jump into our "time machine" and go back to the sixth day of Creation and read what God said to Adam and Eve and the animals:

And God said, Behold, I have given you every herb bearing seed, which is upon the face of all the earth, and every tree, in which is the fruit of a tree yielding seed; to you it shall be for meat. And to every beast of the earth, and to every fowl of the air, and to every thing that creepeth upon the earth, wherein there is life, I have given every green herb for meat: and it was so. And God saw every thing that he had made, and, behold, it was very good. And the evening and the morning were the sixth day (Genesis 1:29-31).

Adam and Eve (and all the animals) were told they were only to eat plants for food. They were all vegetarian. Now don't get worried about the fact that you eat meat today: we will learn later on that everything changed, and God told us in Genesis chapter 9 that we could eat meat — but this was about 1,700 years later.

Originally, when everything was perfect, there were no meat eaters. Adam and Eve weren't frightened of any of the animals; they all lived in perfect harmony. There was no death, disease, suffering, or bloodshed in the world. By the way, when plants are eaten, they don't "die" in the sense that animals do today. In the Hebrew language, animals and humans have a special life principle called a *nephesh*. Plants do not have this, because they are VERY different from animals — plants were given for food. There was no death of animals or humans in the original Creation. As God said, it was *very good*.

At this stage, you may have two questions: Why did animals like *T. rex* have fierce-looking sharp teeth if they were vegetarians? And, why is the world today one in which there is death, disease, suffering, and bloodshed everywhere?

Bible memory verse: *The fear of the LORD is the beginning of wisdom* (Proverbs 9:10).

Ceratosaurus
(ser-ah-toe-SAWR-us), *meaning "horned reptile."*

Deinonychus
(die-NON-i-kus), *meaning "terrible claw."*

Gorilla

Estemmenosuchus
(eh-STEM-en-uh-SOOK-us), *meaning "wreathed with a crown crocodile," was not a true dinosaur, but a therapsid reptile.*

Anurognathus
(an-u-rog-NAY-thus), *meaning "tailless jaw."*

Spider Monkey

19

Here is a question for you to think about. Do animals like *T. rex* (or lions and bears) really have fierce–looking teeth? Or is it just because we know they eat other animals (and sadly sometimes people), and so we automatically think that animals with teeth like theirs must be savage meat eaters?

Now, the truth is that even though bears have teeth like lions and tigers, most bears eat mainly plants and fruits. Some bears are almost totally vegetarian.

Consider the panda. It has really sharp teeth, but it eats mainly plants. The giant panda feeds mainly on bamboo.

Have you ever seen the teeth of a marine iguana? This iguana looks like a savage meat eater — and yet, it is totally a vegetarian.

You see, just because an animal has sharp teeth doesn't mean it's a meat eater. It just means it has sharp teeth!

Tiger

Lion

T. rex

If you've ever helped cut up vegetables when preparing a meal, you'll know that you need a very sharp knife to cut up such things as carrots and potatoes. Obviously, when God made all the animals, He gave them different sorts of teeth, so they could eat a variety of plants and fruits. (Remember the verses in Genesis 1:29–30, where God told Adam and Eve and the animals that their diet would be plants and fruits only.)

Now, it is true that in today's world, a number of different kinds of animals eat other animals. People eat animals, also. Maybe you had chicken or beef for lunch! That's because an event in history changed everything. This event was actually the **saddest day ever** in history. What happened on this day **affected EVERYTHING in the entire universe**. In fact, this event caused **changes for eternity**.

What happened?

Bible memory verse: *For we know that the whole creation groaneth and travaileth in pain together until now* (Romans 8:22).

Panda

Marine Iguana

Bear

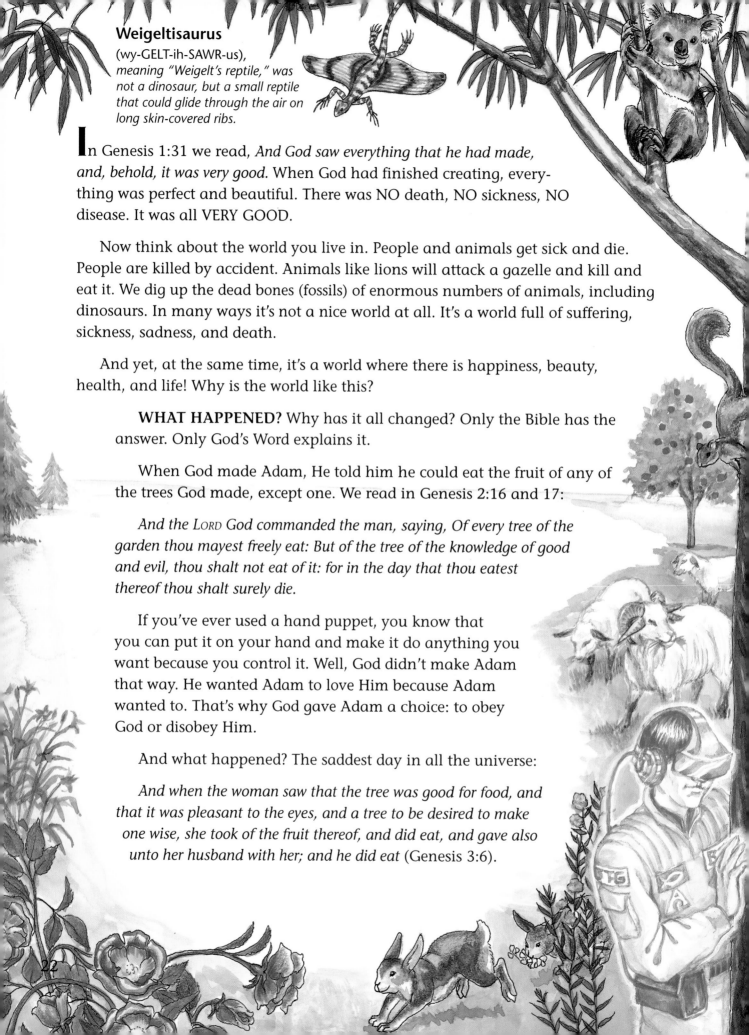

Weigeltisaurus (wy-GELT-ih-SAWR-us), meaning "Weigelt's reptile," was not a dinosaur, but a small reptile that could glide through the air on long skin-covered ribs.

In Genesis 1:31 we read, *And God saw everything that he had made, and, behold, it was very good.* When God had finished creating, everything was perfect and beautiful. There was NO death, NO sickness, NO disease. It was all VERY GOOD.

Now think about the world you live in. People and animals get sick and die. People are killed by accident. Animals like lions will attack a gazelle and kill and eat it. We dig up the dead bones (fossils) of enormous numbers of animals, including dinosaurs. In many ways it's not a nice world at all. It's a world full of suffering, sickness, sadness, and death.

And yet, at the same time, it's a world where there is happiness, beauty, health, and life! Why is the world like this?

WHAT HAPPENED? Why has it all changed? Only the Bible has the answer. Only God's Word explains it.

When God made Adam, He told him he could eat the fruit of any of the trees God made, except one. We read in Genesis 2:16 and 17:

And the LORD God commanded the man, saying, Of every tree of the garden thou mayest freely eat: But of the tree of the knowledge of good and evil, thou shalt not eat of it: for in the day that thou eatest thereof thou shalt surely die.

If you've ever used a hand puppet, you know that you can put it on your hand and make it do anything you want because you control it. Well, God didn't make Adam that way. He wanted Adam to love Him because Adam wanted to. That's why God gave Adam a choice: to obey God or disobey Him.

And what happened? The saddest day in all the universe:

And when the woman saw that the tree was good for food, and that it was pleasant to the eyes, and a tree to be desired to make one wise, she took of the fruit thereof, and did eat, and gave also unto her husband with her; and he did eat (Genesis 3:6).

Adam (our first ancestor) disobeyed God. This is the origin of what the Bible calls "sin." Now, what did God say would happen if Adam disobeyed (sinned)? God said he would *surely die*. In the original Hebrew language, "surely die" is actually a phrase that means "dying you will die." In other words, he would start to die, and eventually die.

This is exactly what happened. Adam started to die the very moment he sinned, and we read in Genesis 5:5 that he died 930 years later.

What has all this to do with dinosaurs?

Bible memory verse: *Wherefore, as by one man sin entered into the world, and death by sin; and so death passed upon all men, for that all have sinned* (Romans 5:12).

Avaceratops
(AY-va-SER-a-tops),
*meaning "Ava
[discoveror's wife]
horn face."*

Euoplocephalus
(you-OP-luh-SEF-uh-lus),
meaning "well-protected head."

The Bible tells us in Romans 8:20–22 that sin affected EVERYTHING God had made. **This means sin affected dinosaurs.** Sin affected plants, the dirt, the stars, each human being. EVERYTHING in the universe.

Why do we find bones of dead dinosaurs?

One of the saddest things to ever happen was that death now entered the world. We need to understand that God is holy, pure, and without sin. Therefore, God couldn't have the same once-perfect relationship with Adam now that he was a sinner. Adam (and all his descendants who would therefore also be sinners, which includes every person who's ever lived) could never live with God in a sinful state.

God judged the world with death. God had to do this because a holy God could not allow a sinful Adam to live. Adam and all his descendants would have to die. Now, because humans are made in God's image (Genesis 1:26), our souls (the real you) will live forever. But as sinners, we would live separated from God forever and ever. Praise God, though; He provided a way that can enable us to be in heaven with God forever.

In the Garden of Eden, God killed an animal, shedding its blood, and clothed Adam and Eve in the animal's skin (Genesis 3:21). Why did God do this?

He was showing Adam and Eve that now there would be death in the world. Not only would people die, but animals, including dinosaurs, would now die, also. Sin affected EVERYTHING.

At the same time, God was showing Adam and Eve that the animal represented a very special person who one day would come and pay the penalty for sin. An animal couldn't take away our sin since we are not connected to the animals, as evolutionists teach. We are made in God's image, very different from the animals. Because a man brought sin into the world, a perfect man was needed to pay the penalty for sin, which was death.

Later in the Bible we read that God sent His Son, the Lord Jesus Christ, who became a perfect man, so He could die on a cross for our sins. He had to die, because death was the penalty for sin given in the Garden of Eden. God the Father showed He accepted Christ's sacrifice as payment for our sin in that He raised the Lord Jesus from the dead. So now, if we come to the Lord Jesus, and *. . . if thou shalt confess with thy mouth the Lord Jesus, and shalt believe in thine heart that God hath raised him from the dead, thou shalt be saved* (Romans 10:9). When we trust in the Lord Jesus, God the Father sees our sins covered by what Jesus did on the Cross. This was the "picture" that God gave Adam and Eve when He clothed them in an animal's skin.

Death is such a sad thing, isn't it? People die and animals die. It's all such a sad world. But what a reminder of the awfulness of sin. And what a reminder of the fact that we need to trust Jesus and confess our sin. Because of sin, everything started to change. People even started to kill other people. One of Adam's children, Cain, murdered his brother. Animals probably started to kill and eat each other. Dinosaurs may have started eating other animals.

For the first time, animals would die on the Earth. It was no longer a perfect world.

But things became even much, much worse!

Bible memory verse: *For as in Adam all die, even so in Christ shall all be made alive* (1 Corinthians 15:22).

Oviraptor
(OH-vi-RAP-tor),
meaning "egg thief."

The Bible tells us in Genesis chapter 3 that thorns and thistles started to grow. God cursed the ground, and it would now be hard for people to work and get food. Because of sin and the Curse, things went from bad to worse.

In Genesis 6:12 we read:

And God looked upon the earth, and, behold, it was corrupt; for all flesh had corrupted his way upon the earth.

Because of sin, people had rebelled against God. *The earth was filled with violence* (Genesis 6:13).

Protoceratops
(PROH-to-SER-a-tops),
meaning "first horned face."

Velociraptor
(vee-LOHS-i-RAP-tor),
meaning "swift robber."

27

But a man called Noah loved God. Imagine what it would have been like if you were Noah. Everyone except your own family had rejected God. There would be wickedness all around you, with people making fun and scoffing at you. Noah must have been a great, godly man to keep his faith in that sort of environment.

Bible memory verse: *But Noah found grace in the eyes of the LORD* (Genesis 6:8).

In Genesis chapter 6 we read that God told Noah He was going to judge the Earth because of the wickedness of man. God was going to destroy the Earth with a Flood that would cover the entire globe. But Noah was instructed by God to build the Ark (an enormous boat that would have been around 437 feet long, 73 feet wide, 44 feet high).

This Ark was to be built to keep Noah's family and two of every (seven of some) kind of land-dwelling, air-breathing animal alive. Noah didn't have to go and collect the animals. God would send them to Noah. What a sight that must have been: first Noah and his three sons building the Ark, and then all the different kinds of land animals coming to Noah to go into the Ark.

By the way, Noah's Ark did not look like some overloaded bathtub with giraffes' necks sticking out of the sides! Noah's Ark was a great barge-like vessel that had plenty of room for Noah, his family, and a large number of animals.

Now read the following verses from the Bible VERY carefully:

And of every living thing of all flesh, two of every sort shalt thou bring into the ark, to keep them alive with thee; they shall be male and female. Of fowls after their kind, and of cattle after their kind, of every creeping thing of the earth after his kind, two of every sort shall come unto thee, to keep them alive (Genesis 6:19–20).

The groups of land animals mentioned above are the same groups listed in Genesis chapter 1 that God created. Dinosaurs must have been included in the groups of

animals God made. Therefore, why would anyone think that dinosaurs were not included with the animals that went on the Ark?

The obvious deduction from the Bible, therefore, is that dinosaurs went on Noah's Ark!

Of course, some people say things like, "but dinosaurs died out millions of years ago." But they couldn't have, as death, bloodshed, disease, and suffering came into the world only after Adam sinned. Remember, Adam was created on Day 6 alongside all the land animals, including dinosaurs, only about 6,000 years ago.

Others say, "But dinosaurs were too big; they wouldn't fit on the Ark."

It is true that some of the skeletons of dinosaurs that have been discovered are huge. For instance, scientists estimate that *T. rex* grew up to 20 feet tall, 50 feet long, and weighed ten tons. One of the largest dinosaurs, *Ultrasaurus*, is estimated to have weighed 55 tons, with a height of 52 feet and a length of 82 feet. The dinosaur *Seismosaurus* is estimated to have been even much larger than this.

But the AVERAGE size of a dinosaur, after considering the skeletons found around the world, is that of a small pony or sheep. Only a few of the dinosaurs grew very large, and even they were once small! Dinosaurs hatched out of eggs, and the largest dinosaur egg found is about the size of a football. So a baby *T. rex* would probably have been small enough to sit on your shoulder!

One of the reasons suggested as to why some dinosaurs were large is because they may have been very old. You see, scientists have observed that many reptiles seem to keep growing well after they have reached the age they can reproduce. The animals that were to be saved on the Ark were going to re-populate the Earth after the Flood. When it came to the very few dinosaur kinds that grew to a very large size, God probably sent "teenagers," NOT "fully grown adults" on the Ark.

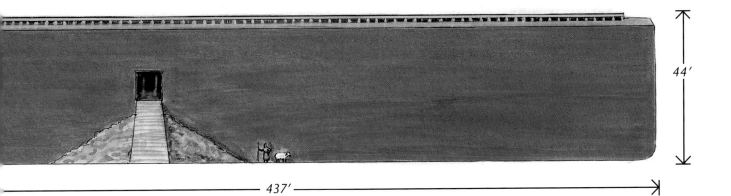

437'   44'

Adult dinosaurs would have been too large to fit comfortably on the Ark. It makes sense that God would have sent younger dinosaurs to the Ark.

Adult Ultrasaurus
(UHL-tra-SAWR-us),
was so nicknamed because of its enormous size. It has not yet received an official scientific name.

Adult Seismosaurus
(SIES-mo-SAWR-us),
meaning "earthquake reptile."

Adult Giraffe

Young Giraffe

Young Ultrasaurus

Some people argue, "But there were too many dinosaurs to fit on the Ark." Although scientists have made up over 600 names of dinosaurs, there were probably less than 50 actual KINDS of dinosaurs. Many of the names are given to just a piece of bone, or a skeleton that looks like another dinosaur but it's a different size, or it's found in a different country.

There is nothing in the Bible that indicates any of the dinosaur kinds died out before the Flood. It's so obvious, two of every kind of dinosaur, which means probably a hundred dinosaurs at the most, were on Noah's Ark, along with all the other kinds of land animals. Drs. Morris and Whitcomb, in their famous book *The Genesis Flood*, and John Woodmorappe in his book *Noah's Ark: a Feasibility Study,* illustrate that there was plenty of room on the Ark for all the different KINDS of land animals.

God's Word tells us that the animals God selected, along with Noah's family, went into the Ark. Seven days later, the Flood started. And what a catastrophe it was!

What happened to the rest of the dinosaurs and other land animals that did NOT go on the Ark?

Bible memory verse: *And Noah did according unto all that the* Lord *commanded him* (Genesis 7:5).

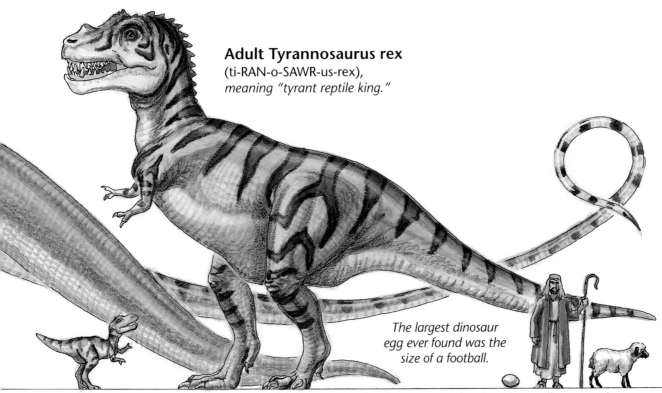

Adult Tyrannosaurus rex
(ti-RAN-o-SAWR-us-rex),
meaning "tyrant reptile king."

The largest dinosaur egg ever found was the size of a football.

Young T. rex

The average size of a dinosaur was the size of a small pony or sheep.

We read in Genesis 7:11–12:

In the six hundredth year of Noah's life, in the second month, the seventeenth day of the month, the same day were all the fountains of the great deep broken up, and the windows of heaven were opened. And the rain was upon the earth forty days and forty nights.

Volcanic eruptions. Earthquakes. Water gushing out from below the Earth's surface. Rain from above. Tidal waves. What do you think happened to the land animals and people that weren't on the Ark?

And all flesh died that moved upon the earth, both of fowl, and of cattle, and of beast, and of every creeping thing that creepeth upon the earth, and every man: All in whose nostrils was the breath of life, of all that was in the dry land, died (Genesis 7:21–22).

All the people and animals that weren't on the Ark drowned. As the water of the Flood gouged out the Earth and deposited great layers of mud over the Earth, plants, animals, and people would be buried.

Corythosaurus
(ko-RITH-o-SAWR-us),
meaning "helmet reptile"

32

As a result, you would expect to find **billions of dead things, buried in rock layers, laid down by water, all over the Earth.** In other words, most of the fossils we find in the Earth's surface are the remains of creatures and plants buried during the time of the Flood. (Some fossils were also formed during the Ice Age which occurred AFTER the Flood.)

Many people think that most fossils are millions of years old. Remember, however, that there was no death of animals or people before sin. As Noah's Flood occurred about 4,500 years ago, that means the fossils from the Flood are only 4,500 years old.

Some people object to this because they think it takes millions of years to turn a dead animal into a fossil. Actually, the process of fossilization can be very quick. In a museum in New Zealand there is on display a "fossil ham." When scientists excavated a village that had been covered by volcanic ash, they found that a ham, left in one of the huts, had petrified. There are many examples similar to this one that show us clearly that to petrify or fossilize something doesn't necessarily take a long time at all.

When you think about it, if animals and plants that die are just left on the ground, they decay into dust. To form a fossil of an animal or plant, they must be covered by lots of mud very quickly, or they'll just disappear. To form millions of fossils in layers that are miles thick in places over the Earth, there had to have been enormous amounts of water and mud. What does this sound like? Noah's Flood, of course!

So eight people (Noah's family), and all the different kinds of land animals, including dinosaurs, were kept safe on the Ark. What happened when the Flood was over?

Bible memory verse: *And the waters prevailed, and were increased greatly upon the earth; and the ark went upon the face of the waters* (Genesis 7:18).

Cryolophosaurus
(cry-o-LOF-o-SAWR-us),
meaning "frozen crested reptile."

We are told in Genesis chapter 8 that the Ark came to rest in the area known as *the mountains of Ararat*. This area today is in the country of Turkey.

Noah's family and all the animals came out of the Ark. This means that two of every dinosaur kind also came out of the Ark, ready to reproduce and spread out across the Earth. Dinosaurs, therefore, must have lived on the Earth after the Flood. People and dinosaurs thus have been living together sometime during the past 4,500 years. Is there any evidence for this?

There's LOTS of evidence.

1. The dragon legends we mentioned earlier were probably based on people's encounters with certain dinosaurs. Certainly, many of the descriptions of these dragons fit the descriptions of known dinosaurs. Consider this description of a "dragon" from an historical account of life in England that describes the animals people saw in A.D. 1405:

    Close to the town of Bures, near Sudbury, there has lately appeared, to the great hurt of the countryside, a dragon, vast in body, with a crested head, teeth like a saw, and a tail extending to an enormous length (*After the Flood* by Bill Cooper, p. 133).

    What do you think this animal might have been? Sounds like a dinosaur to me. This description fits that of a *Dilophosaurus* or *Cryolophosaurus*.

Dilophosaurus
(die-LOF-o-SAWR-us),
meaning "two-crested reptile."

2. There are interesting rock carvings and paintings in different parts of the world that look like dinosaurs. For instance, in Natural Bridges National Monument in Utah, there is a painting made by the Indians that even evolutionists admit looks exactly like a great sauropod dinosaur. Fran Bridges, recognized authority on petroglyphs (rock art) of the American Southwest, stated, "[The] petroglyph . . . bears striking resemblance to a dinosaur, specifically a *Brontosaurus*, with a long tail and neck, small head and all."* Evolutionists won't accept the petroglyph as a dinosaur because they don't believe people lived with dinosaurs. But, they accept other animals the Indians have painted as real animals that they observed. Because of their bias against the Bible, evolutionists won't accept the obvious — Indians saw dinosaurs!

*("Messages on Stone," Creation ex nihilo, Vol. 19 No. 2, p. 23.) Since Fran Bridges made the above statement, the scientific community now knows that Brontosaurus never existed. The confusion came about in 1879 when Othniel Marsh gave the name Brontosaurus to an almost complete skeleton found at Como Bluff, Wyoming, which was missing its skull. In reconstructing the skeleton of this "Brontosaurus," Marsh mistakenly gave it a square-shaped Camarasaurus-type skull found in a nearby quarry. Today, the skeleton's head has been replaced with the longer, narrower type of skull it should have been given originally. The dinosaur's reconstruction has a new name — Apatosaurus.

Utah Indian Petroglyph

Apatosaurus
(a-PAT-o-SAWR-us), meaning "deceptive reptile."

3. There are reports from different parts of the world of large beasts that may actually be living dinosaurs. In the Congo in Central Africa, natives describe a beast they've encountered, and the description fits that of a dinosaur. Some scientists have conducted expeditions to this area and have written books about this mysterious beast. It certainly wouldn't surprise creationists if this really was a living dinosaur!

This is all very fascinating, but there's another, special piece of evidence that indicates dinosaurs lived after the Flood which comes from the Bible. Can you think of any passages in the Bible that might describe a dinosaur living after the Flood?

Bible memory verse: *And God remembered Noah and every living thing, and all the cattle that was with him in the ark* (Genesis 8:1).

Apatosaurus-type skull

Camarasaurus-type skull

Could the strange animal known as the Mokele-Mbembe *(mo-KE-le-MEM-be) that has been sighted in Africa be a sauropod dinosaur such as* Camarasaurus?

Camarasaurus
(KAM-a-ra-SAWR-us), *meaning "chambered reptile."*

37

4. The biblical evidence: Quite some time after the Flood, a man called Job went through a time of testing. After all he went through, Job was reminded by God of how great the Creator was. God talked about many things, including some of the animals that lived at the same time as Job. The following verses are taken from Job chapter 40, as God describes a great animal that Job was familiar with:

Behold now behemoth, which I made with thee; he eateth grass as an ox. Lo now, his strength is in his loins, and his force is in the navel of his belly. He moveth his tail like a cedar: the sinews of his stones are wrapped together. His bones are as strong pieces of brass; his bones are like bars of iron. He is the chief of the ways of God: he that made him can make his sword to approach unto him. Surely the mountains bring him forth food, where all the beasts of the field play. He lieth under the shady trees, in the covert of the reed, and fens. The shady trees cover him with their shadow; the willows of the brook compass him about. Behold, he drinketh up a river, and hasteth not: he trusteth that he can draw up Jordan into his mouth. He taketh it with his eyes: his nose pierceth through snares (Job 40:15–24).

This animal was the *chief of the ways of God*, which means it was the largest land animal God had made. It is also described as having a tail like a cedar tree. Many people have thought that God was describing an elephant or hippopotamus. Does this sound like the description of an elephant or hippopotamus? Do they have tails like a cedar tree? Are they the largest animals that have lived on the Earth? The answer is NO to each of these questions.

As far as we know, one of the dinosaurs was the largest land animal that lived on the Earth. This description fits beautifully one of the sauropod dinosaurs like *Brachiosaurus*. We can't say for sure that the *behemoth* was a dinosaur, but it certainly makes sense that it was.

5. More evidence that dinosaurs lived recently comes from finds of FRESH dinosaur bones. Evolutionists in Montana found parts of a *T. rex* bone that had not fossilized, and it appeared to have red blood cells still present. Now if these bones were millions of years old, there certainly wouldn't be any blood cells left. The more the scientists looked at these bones, the more they were convinced they had really found some blood cells from a *T. rex*. These scientists don't know how to explain this because they don't want to give up their view that the bones are millions of years old.

Dinosaur sculptor and explorer Buddy Davis found unfossilized frozen dinosaur bones in Alaska. Even evolutionists admit these bones wouldn't have been frozen for millions of years. If dinosaur bones really were millions of years old, they should have decayed away or become fossilized! These remains are probably from dinosaurs that lived AFTER the Flood.

If dinosaurs lived after the Flood, and up until relatively recent times when people like Indians saw them, why don't we see dinosaurs today?

What happened to them?

Brachiosaurus
(BRAK-ee-o-SAWR-us), *meaning "arm reptile," averaged 23 feet high at the shoulders.*

Cedar Tree

African elephant averages 10 feet high at the shoulders.

Hippopotamus averages 5 feet high at the shoulders.

Bible memory verse: *Every beast, every creeping thing, and every fowl, and whatsoever creepeth upon the earth, after their kinds, went forth out of the ark (Genesis 8:19).*

Archaeopteryx
(AHR-kee-OP-ter-iks),
meaning "ancient wing."

Lambeosaurus
(LAM-bee-uh-SAWR-us),
meaning "Lambe's [Canadian paleontologist Lawrence Lambe] reptile."

Coelophysis
(SEEL-o-FIE-sis),
meaning "hollow form."

40

Just imagine the terrible scene of destruction Noah must have witnessed when he came out of the Ark after the devastating effects of the Flood. Not only had sin and the Curse affected everything, now the Flood had totally changed the Earth. It must have been a harsh world after the Flood. Volcanoes must have continued to be quite active for some time — there is even some activity now. Earthquakes shook the land. There was not as much food as before the Flood since the plants and trees had been destroyed. It would be harder for man and animals to find something to eat. God knew that things would be very different now. He told Noah:

Every moving thing that liveth shall be meat for you; even as the green herb have I given you all things (Genesis 9:3).

Here we learn that God made a change. Now, because sin entered the world, and because of the effects of the Flood, Noah was told that from that time on, people could eat animals for food. This is why we can eat meat today.

Spinosaurus
(SPINE-o-SAWR-us),
meaning "spiny reptile."

Hypsilophodon
(hip-si-LOF-o-don),
meaning "high-crested tooth."

Euparkeria
(you-park-AIR-ee-ah),
*named in honor of
W.K. Parker, English scientist.*

The Tower of Babel

Tsintaosaurus
(CHING-DOW-SAWR-us),
meaning "reptile from Tsintao."

Gallimimus
(GAL-i-MIME-us),
meaning "fowl mimic."

Of course, animals killing and eating other animals had already begun before the Flood. We find many fossils that show evidence of this. There was also another change God made:

And the fear of you and the dread of you shall be upon every beast of the earth, and upon every fowl of the air, upon all that moveth upon the earth, and upon all the fishes of the sea; into your hand are they delivered (Genesis 9:2).

The relationship between man and the animals was to change. From this time on, the animals would fear man.

Noah's family had children, and they had children, and so people increased in number on the Earth. Some time later, people again rebelled against God and disobeyed His instruction to spread out over the Earth. They congregated to build a tower to worship the heavens, instead of worshiping the God who made the heavens.

42

Stegoceras
(STEG-o-SER-as),
meaning "horny roof."

As a result, God caused these people to speak several different languages, instead of the one language they all had. Because they couldn't work together any more, they spread out over the Earth. As people dispersed, they most likely took some of their favorite animals with them. Perhaps some took dinosaurs. People also built boats and began to sail around the world, also taking animals with them.

A consequence of the processes of the Flood was that an Ice Age began. The northern and southern areas of the Earth became covered in snow and ice. This would have lowered ocean levels and formed land bridges between continents. People and animals, including dinosaurs, probably walked across these land bridges as they spread out over the Earth.

If you want to learn more about the Ice Age, then contact *Answers in Genesis* (the address is at the front of this book) for a great book on this subject.

What has all this to do with what happened to the dinosaurs?

Bible memory verse: *Out of whose womb came the ice?* (Job 38:29).

Dodo Bird
The three known species of the Dodo bird became extinct during the 17th and 18th centuries.

The effects of sin, the Curse, and the Flood caused havoc on the Earth. Now there was competition between man and the animals for food and living space. As people moved out over the Earth, they drove animals out of areas. Famines, floods, volcanic eruptions, earthquakes, and diseases also took their toll on the animals.

Some species of animals (like the Dodo bird) died out completely. In fact, hundreds and hundreds of species of animals have disappeared off the face of the Earth.

This is one of the reasons why many zoos have special "endangered species" programs. If you were to go to a zoo that has such a program and talk to one of the scientists, you might have a conversation something like the following:

Question: "Excuse me, Mr. Scientist, can you tell me why you have an endangered species program?"

Answer: "Why do we have an endangered species program? It's so obvious, isn't it?

"Lots of species of animals have become extinct, like the Australian Eastern Hare Wallaby, which became extinct in 1890; the Indonesian Bali Tiger, which became extinct in 1937; or the Mexican Silver Grizzly, which became extinct in 1964. Scientists estimate that, on average, we lose one to three species of animals every day from the Earth. Lots of animals are on our endangered species list. We've lost thousands of species. We are trying to stop animals becoming extinct."

Indonesian Bali Tiger
became extinct in 1937.

Mexican Silver Grizzly
became extinct in 1964.

Australian Eastern Hare Wallaby
became extinct in 1890.

Pachyrhinosaurus
(PAK-i-RINE-o-SAWR-us),
meaning "thick-nosed reptile."

Question: "Why do animals go extinct?"

Answer: "Why? It should be obvious! Here are just a few of the MANY reasons. Look around the Earth and observe: famines, droughts, floods, fire, diseases, people killing them for food or skins, people destroying their habitats, and animals killing each other. These are just a few of the reasons. Everyone should know these things."

Question: "Well, then, can you tell me what happened to the dinosaurs?"

Answer: "Dinosaurs! What happened to them? We don't know! We haven't really got a clue. It's a mystery! They died out millions of years ago!"

Actually, we DO know what happened to the dinosaurs! Because of sin, the Curse, and the Flood, we now have such things as famines, droughts, floods, fire, diseases, people killing animals, and animals killing each other. In other words, the same reasons that animals become extinct today, are the SAME reasons that dinosaurs died out. And it wasn't millions of years ago; it was probably just hundreds of years ago. There is no mystery whatsoever.

If this is true, why don't the majority of scientists understand this?

A dying **Diplodocus** (di-PLOD-o-kus), *meaning "double beam."*

47

Dinosaur   *Archaeopteryx*   Modern Bird

EVOLUTION OF DINOSAURS TO BIRDS

*Some evolutionists have claimed **Archaeopteryx** (ark-ee-OP-ter-ix) was a part-dinosaur/part-bird mix. They have said it had teeth and clawed fingers like a reptile, as well as feathers and wings like a bird. Teeth are meaningless, however, for not all dinosaurs had teeth, nor do all living reptiles have them. Also, there are living birds with claws on their wings — the South American hoatzin, the African touraco, and the ostrich. Archaeopteryx may have been unusual, but it was 100 percent bird.*

The reason most scientists don't know what happened to the dinosaurs is because they've been brainwashed to believe in "molecules–to–man" evolution. For them, life began in the sea millions of years ago; somehow, chemicals turned into life. They believe that over millions of years, one kind of animal slowly changed into a different kind of animal. The fossil record is supposedly the record of this evolutionary process.

Their evolutionary view teaches that dinosaurs allegedly evolved around 200 million years ago. They ruled the Earth for millions of years and then suddenly died out about 65 million years ago.

Evolutionists don't have a "time machine" to know what happened in the past. They weren't there, so they have to make guesses as to what they think happened. All they have are living animals and plants, and lots of dead ones in the fossil record. When they dig up fossils, they don't dig up a history book that tells them what happened.

Now, we do have a history book (the Bible) that does tell us all we need to know about the events of the past. And as you've seen, when we use that history book, we can make sense of the world. We can understand why there are fossils all over the Earth. The Bible explains why there is death in the world. And an understanding of the true history of the world enables us to explain all about dinosaurs.

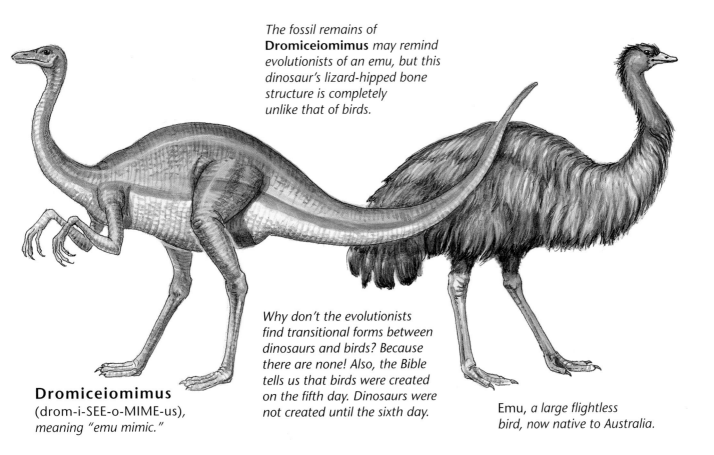

The fossil remains of **Dromiceiomimus** *may remind evolutionists of an emu, but this dinosaur's lizard-hipped bone structure is completely unlike that of birds.*

Dromiceiomimus
(drom-i-SEE-o-MIME-us),
meaning "emu mimic."

Why don't the evolutionists find transitional forms between dinosaurs and birds? Because there are none! Also, the Bible tells us that birds were created on the fifth day. Dinosaurs were not created until the sixth day.

Emu, *a large flightless bird, now native to Australia.*

By the way, if evolution were true, you would expect to find in the fossil record evidence of in-between or transitional forms, as one kind of animal changed into a totally different kind of animal. But you don't find any such things! Dinosaurs, for instance, have **always** been dinosaurs.

But, evolutionists believe that dinosaurs evolved into birds. Once they thought they found a fossil dinosaur with feathers on it in China. If such a fossil really existed, they could say it was a transitional form. But when they studied the fossil closely, they found out it didn't have feathers at all. A different fossil that actually had feathers was found to be part of a bird fossil that had been glued together with part of a dinosaur one! But, evolutionists are so convinced there is no God and that the Bible is not true, they even say that hummingbirds are dinosaurs (*The Great Dinosaur Mystery Solved!* by Ken Ham, p. 74–77)!

If the Bible explains dinosaurs (as well as everything else we observe in the world) so simply, why don't the majority of scientists believe the Bible? Why do they cling to evolution?

Bible memory verse: *All flesh is not the same flesh: but there is one kind of flesh of men, another flesh of beasts, another of fishes, and another of birds* (1 Corinthians 15:39).

The Bible has the answer. If we get into our "time machine" once again, and go back to the Garden of Eden by reading Genesis chapter 3, we find that Adam sinned because he didn't accept what God told him to do. Adam thought he could decide truth for himself instead of listening to God's Word.

Now because we are descendants of Adam, we are sinners just like him. Romans 3:23 states: *For all have sinned, and come short of the glory of God.* Each one of us is just like Adam. Our very nature is such that we don't really want to listen to God's Word.

That's why we are so easily led astray by evolutionists teaching such things as millions of years of history. Down deep in our hearts, we would rather listen to the fallible scientists' opinions than the clear Word of God.

Inostrancevia
(in-OS-tran-SEV-ee-ah),
named after Russian paleontologist Aleksandr Inostrancev. Inostrancevia was not a true dinosaur, but a therapsid reptile

Carnotaurus
(KAHR-no-TAWR-us),
meaning "meat-eating bull."

Psittacosaurus
(si-TAK-o-SAWR-us),
meaning "parrot reptile."

51

Peter gives an example of this in 2 Peter 3:5. He states: *For this they willingly are ignorant of, that by the word of God the heavens were of old, and the earth standing out of the water and in the water: Whereby the world that then was, being overflowed with water, perished.*

Take note of the phrase *willingly are ignorant of* (or deliberately reject). This means they don't WANT to believe. Young people often ask the question, "If there's so much evidence for the Flood all over the Earth, and if it's so obvious God created, and the Bible is true, wouldn't the scientists surely believe these things?"

The answer is that scientists, like everyone else, are sinners. Because of this, they don't want to believe. It has **nothing** to do with the evidence. There is an exception, of course, for those whose hearts have been changed by the Holy Spirit, becoming true Christians. Sadly though, most people today are in rebellion against God, just as in Noah's day.

Peter also tells us in 2 Peter 3:7 that just as surely as God sent the Flood as a judgment, so there is going to be another judgment, but not by water. Next time the judgment will be by fire. And this will be the FINAL judgment.

What will happen to the Earth when this judgment occurs?

Bible memory verse: *But the heavens and the earth, which are now, by the same word are kept in store, reserved unto fire against the day of judgment and perdition of ungodly men* (2 Peter 3:7).

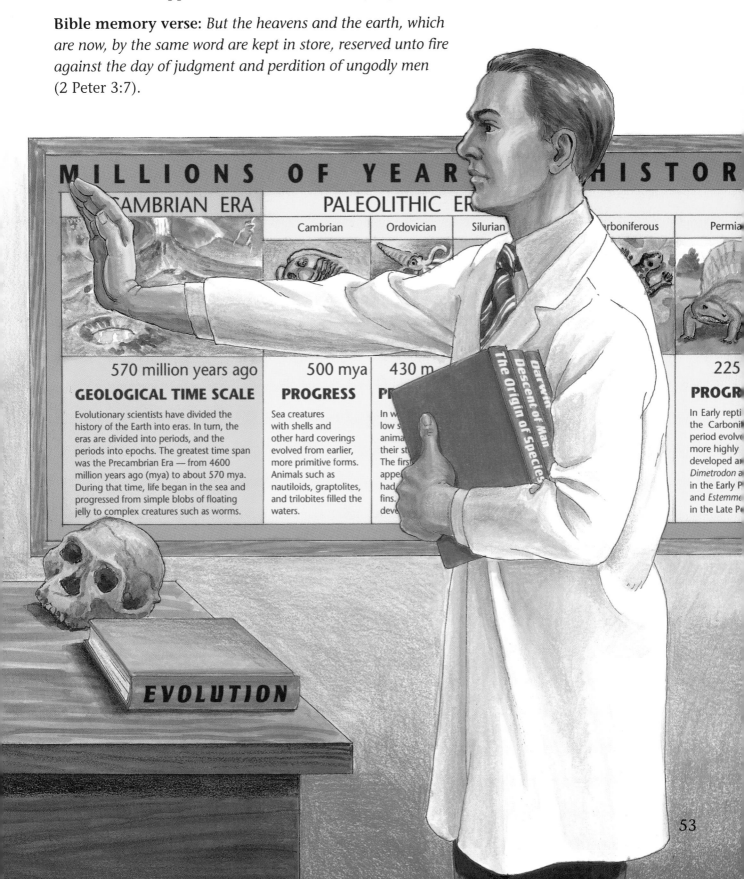

MILLIONS OF YEAR HISTOR

CAMBRIAN ERA

PALEOLITHIC ER

| Cambrian | Ordovician | Silurian | rboniferous | Permia |

570 million years ago

GEOLOGICAL TIME SCALE

Evolutionary scientists have divided the history of the Earth into eras. In turn, the eras are divided into periods, and the periods into epochs. The greatest time span was the Precambrian Era — from 4600 million years ago (mya) to about 570 mya. During that time, life began in the sea and progressed from simple blobs of floating jelly to complex creatures such as worms.

500 mya

PROGRESS

Sea creatures with shells and other hard coverings evolved from earlier, more primitive forms. Animals such as nautiloids, graptolites, and trilobites filled the waters.

430 m

P

In w
low s
anima
their st
The firs
appe
had
fins.
dev

225

PROGR

In Early repti
the Carboni
period evolve
more highly
developed a
Dimetrodon a
in the Early P
and *Estemme*
in the Late P

Darwin
Descent of Man
The Origin of Species

EVOLUTION

Peter tells us that . . . *the heavens shall pass away with a great noise, and the elements shall melt with fervent heat, the earth also and the works that are therein shall be burned up* (2 Peter 3:10). We're told in Isaiah that . . . *the host of heaven shall be dissolved, and the heavens shall be rolled together as a scroll: and all their host shall fall down, as the leaf falleth off from the vine, and as a falling fig from the fig tree* (Isaiah 34:4).

But the good news is that God is going to make . . . *new heavens and a new earth, wherein dwelleth righteousness* (2 Peter 3:13).

And there's even more good news! God is going to remove the Curse, and there will be no more death, disease and suffering. Just as it was in the Garden of Eden before sin.

And there shall be no more curse (Revelation 22:3).

And God shall wipe away all tears from their eyes; and there shall be no more death, neither sorrow, nor crying, neither shall there be any more pain: for the former things are passed away (Revelation 21:4).

And if there are animals on this new Earth, what will they be like? Isaiah 11:6–9 seems to give us a glimpse of what this future state will be like:

The wolf also shall dwell with the lamb, and the leopard shall lie down with the kid; and the calf and the young lion and the fatling together; and a little child shall lead them. And the cow and the bear shall feed; their young ones shall lie down together: and the lion shall eat straw like the ox. And the sucking child shall play on the hole of the asp, and the weaned child shall put his hand on the cockatrice's den. They shall not hurt nor destroy in all my holy mountain: for the earth shall be full of the knowledge of the LORD, as the waters cover the sea.

This sounds as if it will be just as it was in the Garden of Eden before sin: the animals and humans living together in perfect harmony. They're vegetarians.

But what is going to happen to all the people who have ever died, and those who will still be alive when the final judgment comes? What will happen to you and me?

Bible memory verse: *And I saw a new heaven and a new earth: for the first heaven and the first earth were passed away; and there was no more sea* (Revelation 21:1).

In the last book of the Bible, Revelation, our "time machine" gives us some details about the future. We are told that everyone who has ever lived will stand before God to give an account of his or her life:

And I saw the dead, small and great, stand before God; and the books were opened: and another book was opened, which is the book of life: and the dead were judged out of those things which were written in the books, according to their works (Revelation 20:12).

John, who wrote the Book of Revelation (directed by God's Holy Spirit, of course), told us that some people are going to live with God in heaven forever:

And I heard a great voice out of heaven saying, Behold, the tabernacle of God is with men, and he will dwell with them, and they shall be his people, and God himself shall be with them, and be their God (Revelation 21:3). John then says death, sorrow and pain will be no more.

Sadly, though, John tells us that many people will be sent to everlasting punishment:

And whosoever was not found written in the book of life was cast into the lake of fire (Revelation 20:15).

We get even more details about those who cannot live with God:

But the fearful, and unbelieving, and the abominable, and murderers, and whoremongers, and sorcerers, and idolaters, and all liars, shall have their part in the lake which burneth with fire and brimstone: which is the second death (Revelation 21:8).

At this stage, everyone reading this book should be asking the question, "Where am I going to spend eternity?" Did you know that thinking back over all we've learned about dinosaurs helps us answer the question?

Bible memory verse: *And, behold, I come quickly; and my reward is with me, to give every man according as his work shall be* (Revelation 22:12).

Plateosaurus
(PLAT-ee-o-SAWR-us),
meaning "flat reptile."

Sauropelta
(SAWR-o-PEL-ta),
meaning "shield reptile."

Imagine you have a dinosaur bone in front of you. What lesson can you learn from this piece of dead bone? Think back about our "time machine" travels.

Dinosaurs were created on the sixth day of Creation, the same day Adam and Eve were created. But Adam and Eve were very different from the dinosaurs and other animals — they were made in the image of God.

Dinosaurs, as well as the other animals, originally lived in perfect harmony with Adam and Eve. All were vegetarian. There was no death, disease, and bloodshed in the world. However, Adam sinned against God and everything changed: *For the wages of sin is death* (Romans 6:23).

As a result, death, disease, bloodshed, and suffering entered the world. Thus, dinosaurs and people began to die. Because all people are descendants of Adam and Eve, all people are sinners: *For all have sinned, and come short of the glory of God* (Romans 3:23).

58

Amargasaurus
(am-MAHR-gah-SAWR-us),
*named after La Amarga Creek,
in Argentina, where found.*

Okapi

Dimetrodon
(die-ME-truh-don),
*meaning "two-measure tooth,"
was not a true dinosaur,
but a synapsid reptile.*

59

Because of the wickedness of man, God judged the world with a global flood. However, Noah's family and representatives of all the land animals, including dinosaurs, were saved on the Ark. Dinosaurs that weren't on the Ark died — that's why we find so many dead bones over the Earth. It's a reminder of God's judgment of sin.

The Ark is really a picture of how we can be saved from our sin. Just as Noah went through the door of the Ark to be saved, so we must also go through a door — that door is the Lord Jesus Christ: *I am the door: by me if any man enter in, he shall be saved* (John 10:9). Because a man (Adam) brought sin and death into the world, so a perfect man (Jesus) was needed to pay for our sin: *For God so loved the world, that he gave his only begotten Son, that whosoever believeth in him should not perish, but have everlasting life* (John 3:16).

God's Son became a man (He was the "God-man") so that He could die on a cross for our sins. He was raised from the dead, showing that the penalty for sin was paid: *But God commendeth his love toward us, in that, while we were yet sinners, Christ died for us* (Romans 5:8).

How can we be saved from our sin? *That if thou shalt confess with thy mouth the Lord Jesus, and shalt believe in thine heart that God hath raised him from the dead, thou shalt be saved* (Romans 10:9).

Polacanthus
(pol-a-KAN-thus),
meaning "many spines."

Parasaurolophus
(PAR-a-SAWR-o-LOH-fus),
*meaning "similar
crested reptile."*

*Komodo
Dragons*

61

Is that **all** we have to do? *For by grace are ye saved through faith; and that not of yourselves: it is the gift of God: Not of works, lest any man should boast* (Ephesians 2:8–9). Our good works won't get us to heaven. We need to accept God's free gift of salvation to us, and then we will want to do good works.

How can we be sure we are saved and will go to heaven? *These things have I written unto you that believe on the name of the Son of God; that ye may know that ye have eternal life, and that ye may believe on the name of the Son of God* (1 John 5:13).

Bible memory verses: All of the above verses are important to memorize.

Did dinosaurs go to heaven?

Dinosaurs are animals. They're not made in the image of God. They don't have an immortal soul as every human being does. The Bible tells us that an animal's "soul" returns to the dust of the Earth. However, a human soul lives on for ever and ever.

Is there any other way to be saved so we can go to heaven?

Read these verses from the Bible very carefully:

Jesus saith unto him, I am the way, the truth, and the life: no man cometh unto the Father, but by me (John 14:6).

Neither is there salvation in any other: for there is none other name under heaven given among men, whereby we must be saved (Acts 4:12).

God's Word teaches us that you can be the nicest person in the world, doing great things for people, but if you don't trust in the Lord Jesus Christ, you can't go to heaven.

In John chapter 3, we read about a man called Nicodemus who came to talk to Jesus. The Lord had a special message for Nicodemus, one that applies to each one of us:

. . . Verily, verily, I say unto thee, Except a man be born again, he cannot see the kingdom of God (John 3:3).

That's why it is so important that you have confessed your sins and accepted the free gift of salvation that Jesus offers. If you've never done this, then why not do it now? Why don't you pray the following prayer on this book's last page, if you mean it?

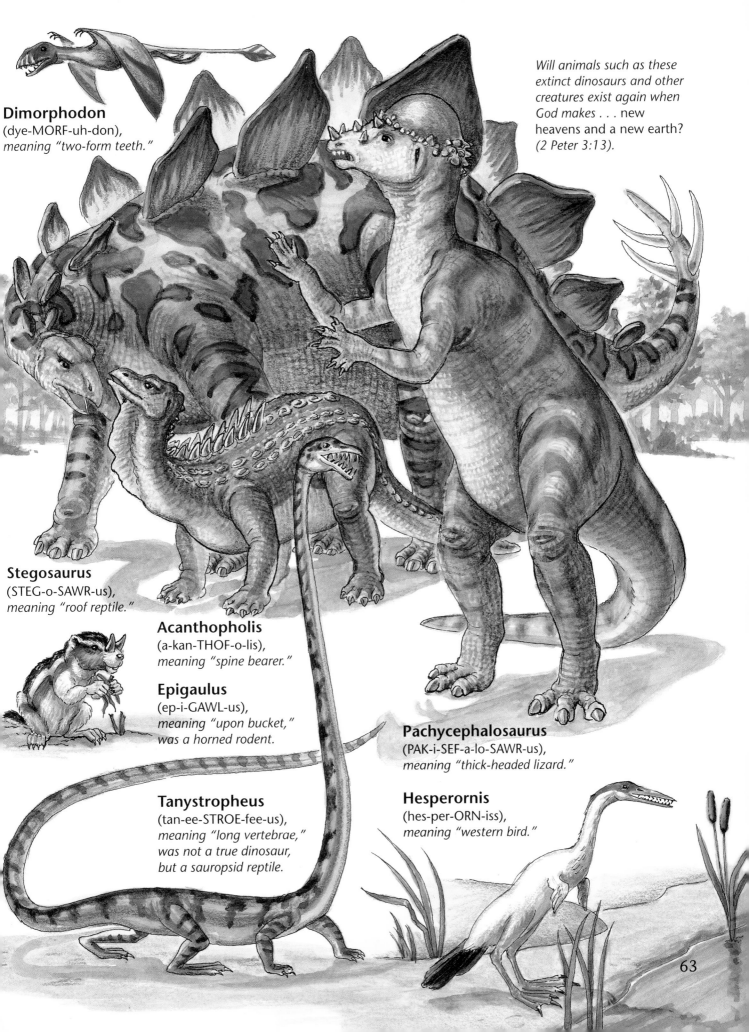

Dimorphodon
(dye-MORF-uh-don),
meaning "two-form teeth."

*Will animals such as these
extinct dinosaurs and other
creatures exist again when
God makes . . . new
heavens and a new earth?
(2 Peter 3:13).*

Stegosaurus
(STEG-o-SAWR-us),
meaning "roof reptile."

Acanthopholis
(a-kan-THOF-o-lis),
meaning "spine bearer."

Epigaulus
(ep-i-GAWL-us),
*meaning "upon bucket,"
was a horned rodent.*

Pachycephalosaurus
(PAK-i-SEF-a-lo-SAWR-us),
meaning "thick-headed lizard."

Tanystropheus
(tan-ee-STROE-fee-us),
*meaning "long vertebrae,"
was not a true dinosaur,
but a sauropsid reptile.*

Hesperornis
(hes-per-ORN-iss),
meaning "western bird."

Dear Lord Jesus, I recognize that I am a sinner in rebellion against my Creator. I know that You are the Son of God. You died on the Cross for my sins. I don't deserve what You did for me. But I want to love You and ask You to forgive my sins and remember them no more as Your Word promised. Thank You for saving me for eternity. Help me to now live my life as I should. Show me from Your Word what I should do with my life. Thank You, Lord Jesus. Amen.

Here are two Bible passages to challenge you:

Wherewithal shall a young man cleanse his way? By taking heed thereto according to thy word (Psalm 119:9).

Study to shew thyself approved unto God, a workman that needeth not to be ashamed, rightly dividing the word of truth (2 Timothy 2:15).

You need to start studying THE HISTORY BOOK OF THE UNIVERSE, the Bible, starting at the beginning with Genesis in the Old Testament. Of course, you need to read the whole Bible over and over again. However, to find more details about salvation, be sure to read the New Testament with the Old, beginning with the gospels — Matthew, Mark, Luke, and John.

And please, write to us at *Answers in Genesis* to tell us that you committed your life to the Lord Jesus Christ.

Do you think God will ever make dinosaurs again so we will see them in the new Earth? I hope so, don't you?

Bible memory verse: *Thy word is true from the beginning* (Psalm 119:160).

Maiasaura
*(MAY-ya-SAWR-a),
meaning "good mother
reptile."*